LEADER GUIDE
VIDEO AND AUDIO APPLICATION

JOHN C. MAXWELL

DEVELOPING the LEADER WITHIN YOU

Need More Workbooks?

Visit
www.INJOY.com

Or call
1-800-333-6506

Dear Friend,

What a privilege—you have the opportunity to impact people's lives.

You are preparing to give your time to developing other people. And even as you are equipping others, you will become an even stronger leader and more impacting influencer yourself!

You and I are going to be partners over the next few weeks and months. You will see your leadership ability growing as you just listen, learn and complete the exercises for yourself. But as you teach what you are learning, you will find that you experience a new level of understanding and growth.

Before each section, I have included a page for you with some ideas on how to lead a group through this information. I believe that there are four essential elements of effective teaching:

- *Introducing the lesson*
- *Watching the lesson*
- *Group discussion*
- *Challenge*

We have included some ideas for you in each of these areas to make your teaching experience as simple as possible.

I have devoted my life to equipping leaders and it is my hope that this resource will enable you to equip others effectively as you become the leader you have always dreamed of becoming.

Your friend,

John C. Maxwell

Developing the Leader Within You

Leader Guide

Table of Contents

Developing the Leader Within You

Leader Guide

The Leader's Role

It is imperative that you, as the facilitator, become totally familiar with all of the material in this application series. Audiotapes of the videos have been included to make it more convenient for you to study the material. We recommend several reviews of each lesson, so be sure to allow enough preparation time for these reviews. Each lesson is 25–35 minutes long, and remember to leave time to stop the tape as you capture ideas for your class.

Facilitators are encouraged to complete and study all exercises, as well as look for ways to tailor them to their particular group. You should emphasize to each participant that all exercises should be consistently performed to ensure that maximum benefits from the course are attained.

We would like to stress this point…detailed preparation by the facilitator in terms of course content and leadership is the most vital element for the success of this course.

As you begin to study the course content, you will realize that your task as facilitator will be challenging and essential. This Guide is designed to provide a framework, but the safeguard for mastery of content is up to you! Only you can:

- Ensure that the key concepts are understood

- Facilitate the individual and group exercises

- Inspire meaningful discussion

- Initiate content application

  and most importantly,

- Establish an environmental atmosphere for learning and change.

Preparation should be somewhat unique for each facilitator, but we can recommend a proven strategy: spend time in planning, preparation, and practice.

Overview

As the facilitator, you must be very familiar with this information—take the time to prepare. You have the flexibility to add group discussion questions, group exercises and apply other teaching techniques to tailor the course to your individual group.

Each of the lessons in this Leader Guide is broken into four elements to assist you in preparing and presenting this course.

1. **Introduce the Lesson**   *(Approximately 5 minutes)*
   This section will give you ideas and prepare you for introducing the lesson.

2. **Watch the Lesson**   *(Approximately 25–35 minutes)*
   As a group, watch the lesson that John Maxwell presents.

3. **Group Discussion**   *(Approximately 15 minutes)*
   This will usually include discussion questions to reinforce lesson materials.

4. **Challenge**   *(Approximately 5 minutes)*
   Now it's time to send them off and challenge them to apply their new information.

Preparation

Step 1: Read the book *Developing the Leader Within You*
(to order: **www.INJOY.com** / 1-800-333-6506).

Step 2: Watch the videos.

Step 3: Listen to the audiotapes.

Step 4: Study all elements of this Guide and the Student Workbook.

Step 5: Teach yourself the class. Go through each element just as your students will.

Step 6: Make sure that you have a workbook for each person in your group
(to order: **www.INJOY.com** / 1-800-333-6506).

Step 7: Study your group make-up. Try to anticipate their expectations and make notes on points you want to tailor or emphasize, develop additional discussion questions, etc.

Helpful Hints

1. Begin each session on time.

2. If you don't show excitement and enthusiasm for the course, don't expect your students to be very inspired.

3. Communicate the importance of the group discussions and exercises.

4. Create a climate of participation. Let everyone know they can contribute to others' learning.

5. Don't be afraid of silence. People need time to digest thoughts, especially new ones.

6. Encourage multiple answers for each discussion question.

7. Avoid asking yes and no questions.

8. Avoid answering your own questions.

9. Probe thoughts with spontaneous follow-up questions.

10. Reinforce the value of contributions made by participants.

11. End each session on time.

12. **And always have fun!**

Room Setup

The physical setup of the room is a very important factor in a successful (or unsuccessful) course presentation. The best, most stimulating presentation imaginable will fail if the participants are unable to see, hear or sit comfortably. Not all aspects of the setup will be within the control of the facilitator, but here are some things to consider.

Room Size... Note taking and group exercises are important elements of this program. Make sure adequate space is available to support these activities.

Seating... This course is designed around eighteen classes averaging about one hour. Comfortable seating is important. Your seating plan should allow everyone to comfortably see any flip chart or writing board used in the class.

Room Temperature... This factor is often overlooked. Know how to correct this situation if it becomes an issue.

Facilitator's Notes... A flip chart, board or overhead projector should be provided for the facilitator's use to reinforce points and complete some of the programmed activities of this class. Make sure you have enough fresh pens with plenty of ink in them.

Identification... Name plates/tents can be placed on the participants' tables. This greatly assists the facilitator's interaction with the participants. Individual name badges are also recommended for groups that have guests and/or where individuals are not familiar with one another.

Materials... Any participants' lesson materials should be placed at each seat with a writing instrument. We suggest no additional note taking materials be provided. Encourage all notes be made in the lesson notes you provided.

Lesson One

What is a Leader?

Part One Overview

Introduce the Lesson *(5 minutes)*

Leader, this first time together will be a lot of fun! Set a warm and personal tone from the beginning so that it will break down any barriers to participation. If the participants in your group don't know each other, some sort of a "get to know you" activity to open with is recommended. Because you want openness throughout this course, it is important that everyone feel comfortable with each other.

Let your group know that it is all right NOT to be a great leader. Everyone has room to grow in this area and you are all in it together. Share some of the areas you are hoping to grow in.

The basic principles of leadership are taught in this lesson and the next—share briefly what you have already learned from going through this portion of the course.

Watch the Lesson *(25–35 minutes)*

Make sure everyone is comfortable and can see the screen easily; then show the video.

Group Discussion *(15 minutes)*

1. Ask several students to comment on a recurring theme they heard throughout this session.

2. Ask participants to share a personal experience about how they have been equipped by a leader.

3. Ask participants to share if anything was new or confusing to them.

Challenge *(5 minutes)*

One of the best ways to ensure that your group is learning is to make sure they are applying the lessons on their own time. Every week, you want to challenge your group to take action on what they have learned.

For this first lesson, outside of completing the **Stop and Assess** exercises from the notes, the best challenge is to just have them prepare for the rest of this course. For example:

- Make sure everyone has a *Developing the Leader Within You* book and a Student Workbook. If not, ask them to get one of each this week.

- Have them start reading *Developing the Leader Within You.*

- Make sure they mark their calendars for all future meetings.

Lesson One

What is a Leader?

Part One

 In this section, you will learn the bottom line meaning of leadership and the characteristics of a good leader.

When I see a **LEADER**, *I think of the word...*

L EADERSHIP _____

E

A

D

E

R

Myths of Leadership

1. Leaders are _____ BORN _____ , not _____ MADE _____ .

2. Leadership is a _____ RARE SKILL _____ .

3. Leadership exists only at the _____ TOP _____ of an organization.

    Leadership is _____ INFLUENCE _____ , not position.

4. That all leaders are _____ CHARISMATIC _____ in personality.

    _____ CHARISMA _____ will get you inside the door.

    _____ CREDIBILITY _____ will keep you there.

5. Leaders control by _____ MANIPULATION _____ .

    Manipulation—Moving people for the _____ LEADER'S _____ advantage.

    Motivation—Moving people for _____ EVERYONE'S _____ advantage.

STOP and Assess

The following questions will give you insight about your beliefs concerning leadership:

1. Do any of the above myths describe your personal beliefs about leadership?

2. On which myths do you personally most often operate?

The Making of a Leader

1. Understand the _____VALUE_____ of leadership.

> ## Everything rises and falls on leadership!

2. Make a _____COMMITMENT_____ to learn how to lead.

This will affect the size of your organization.

If you spend one hour a day for five years on
any given subject, you will become an expert in that field.

—Earl Nightengale

Growth stops when the price gets too high.

Becoming a leader will cost you…

(1) _____PERSONAL CHANGE_____

(2) _____TIME_____

(3) _____DOLLARS_____

(4) _____FRIENDSHIPS_____

(5) _____YOUR OPTIONS AND YOUR FREEDOM_____

 **and Assess**

> Non-growing organizations are a result of non-growing leaders. Name at least three things you have done in the past year to help you grow in your leadership position.
>
> (1) _____
>
> (2) _____
>
> (3) _____

 **THIS**

To persevere in strengthening your leadership skills is to continually grow. Like a great athlete, musician or skilled surgeon, your skills will not develop overnight. Days, weeks, months and years of steady striving lead you to achieve the goal. A persistent march toward the pursuit of solid leadership will yield solid results. Leadership is a life-long process.

President Theodore Roosevelt was a great example of a man who always reached for the next step. At the time of his death, then Vice President Marshall said, *Death had to take him sleeping, for if Roosevelt had been awake, there would have been a fight.* When they removed him from his bed, they found a book under his pillow. Even at the end of life, Roosevelt was striving to learn and improve himself.

 **and Assess**

> Are you committed to growth? Take a few minutes to answer the following questions. These will help you determine your real commitment to growth.
>
> 1. What will it cost you to make a commitment to learn how to lead?
>
> 2. Are you willing to carve your schedule in such a way that you allow time to learn how to be a true leader?
>
> 3. What personal habits in your life are helping you become a better leader?
>
> 4. What personal habits in your life hinder you from becoming a better leader?

3. _____START_____ leading.

Leadership can be described on **FOUR LEVELS:**

(1) Leadership that _____INTERESTS_____ people—"I know where I'm going."

(2) Leadership that _____IMPRESSES_____ people—"I've been there."

(3) Leadership that _____INFLUENCES_____ people—"I have taken you with me."

(4) Leadership that _____IMPACTS_____ people—"You have taken others with you."

 **STOP** *and Assess*

Where are you taking people? Have you been there before? Answer the following questions to help you see where you've been and where you're going.

1. When you're the driver of the car, it's vital that you know where you're going. The same applies to leadership. Where are you going with your dreams, ideas and visions? Can you see the end?

2. Have you done the work in the trenches to say to others, *I've been through this and I'm going to lead you through it?*

3. Do you lead in such a way that you are investing in people, giving them confidence and the ability to lead others?

Now that you've checked your directional angle, what steps can you take to help stay on track and take others with you?

When I see a **LEADER***, I think of the word...*

LEADERSHIP

E QUIPPER _____

A

D

E

R

It is only as we develop others that we permanently succeed.

—Harvey S. Firestone

An Equipper's Gameplan

1. Develop _____ SELF _____
2. _____ LEAD _____ self
3. _____ DEVELOP _____ others
4. _____ LEAD _____ others
5. Lead others to develop _____ OTHERS _____
6. Lead others to _____ LEAD _____ others

E VALUATE
How well can they do? 1 to 10

| poor | 1 | 2 | 3 | 4 | 5 | 6 | 7 | 8 | 9 | 10 | excellent |

Q UALIFY
How well did they do? 1 to 10

| poor | 1 | 2 | 3 | 4 | 5 | 6 | 7 | 8 | 9 | 10 | excellent |

U NITE
How well are we doing together? 1 to 10

| poor | 1 | 2 | 3 | 4 | 5 | 6 | 7 | 8 | 9 | 10 | excellent |

I NVEST TIME
Is my time with them profitable? 1 to 10

| poor | 1 | 2 | 3 | 4 | 5 | 6 | 7 | 8 | 9 | 10 | excellent |

P ROVIDE RESOURCES AND EXPERIENCES
Am I providing resources and experiences to help them? 1 to 10

| poor | 1 | 2 | 3 | 4 | 5 | 6 | 7 | 8 | 9 | 10 | excellent |

When I see a **LEADER**, *I think of the word…*

LEADERSHIP

EQUIPPER

A TTITUDE _____

D

E

R

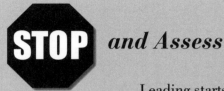 **and Assess**

Leading starts with self. Answer the following questions to determine if you—the leader—have a heart for others.

1. In what ways do you encourage other people? Do you quickly notice the right they have done or the wrong?

2. Do people know that you genuinely care about them? Why or why not?

3. Do you invest time in people as you try to equip them?

The following are important things to remember about motivating and de-motivating people. Read them carefully and work to incorporate them into your leadership.

What motivates people:

Significant contributions—People want to belong to a group or pursue a cause that will have lasting impact.

Goal participation—People support what they create. Allow people to have input and work toward completion of a goal.

Positive dissatisfaction—Dissatisfaction can inspire change or create a critical spirit. The key is to direct dissatisfaction toward positive, effective change.

What de-motivates people:

Criticism—Public criticism hurts! Stay alert and be sensitive to the feelings of others.

Manipulation—Manipulation tears down the walls of trust in a relationship. Honesty and transparency yield better results than crafty maneuvering tactics.

Insensitivity—Make people your priority. Learn to listen without being pre-occupied and in a hurry. Let others know that you care.

Discouraging personal growth—Encourage your staff to stretch and grow. Give them opportunities to succeed. Don't discourage growth because you may feel threatened by the success of others.

As a leader, your tendency to motivate or de-motivate is your choice. Which style will characterize you?

As you reflect on your leadership style, list at least two of your traits that motivate others:

1. _____

2. _____

Now list at least two of your traits that de-motivate people:

1. _____

2. _____

How can you reverse the de-motivators?

_____

_____

Attitude

The longer I live, the more I realize the impact of attitude on life.
Attitude to me is more important than facts.
It is more important than the past,
is more important than education, than money,
than circumstances, than failures, than successes,
than what other people think, or say or do.
It is more important than appearance, giftedness or skill.

It will make or break a company, a church, a home.
The remarkable thing is we have a choice every day
regarding the attitude we will embrace for that day.
We cannot change our past —
We cannot change the fact that people will act in a certain way.
We cannot change the inevitable.

The only thing we can do is play on that one string we have,
and that is our attitude.
I am convinced that life is 10% what happens to me and
90% how I react to it.

—Charles Swindoll

What Is an Attitude?

It is the "advance man" of our true selves.
Its roots are inward but its fruit is outward.
It is our best friend or our worst enemy.
It is more honest and more consistent than our words.
It is an outward look based on past experiences.
It is a thing which draws people to us or repels them.
It is never content until it is expressed.
It is the librarian of our past.
It is the speaker of our present.
It is the prophet of our future.

—John C. Maxwell, *The Winning Attitude*

 *and Assess*

A leader who stays on top will possess a winning and tenacious attitude. Successful leaders have good attitudes about themselves, others and life.

Check your attitude with the following questions.

Our Attitudes that Determine our Capacity to Lead Others

1. Do you welcome responsibility?

2. Do other people's failures annoy us or challenge us?

3. Do we use people or cultivate people?

4. Do we direct people or develop people?

5. Do we criticize or encourage?

6. Do we shun the problem person or seek him out?

7. Do you nurse resentments or do you readily forgive injuries done to you?

8. Are you reasonably optimistic?

9. Do you possess tact? Can you anticipate the likely effect of a statement before you make it?

10. Do your subordinates appear at ease in your presence?

11. Are you unduly dependent on the praise or approval of others?

12. Do you find it easy to make and keep friends?

13. Can you accept opposition to your viewpoint or decision without considering it a personal affront and reacting accordingly?

14. Can you induce people to do happily some legitimate thing which they would not normally wish to do?

15. Are you entrusted with the handling of difficult and delicate situations?

16. Do you possess the ability to secure discipline without having to resort to a show of authority?

17. Do your readily secure the cooperation and win the respect and confidence of others?

18. Can you use disappointments creatively?

19. Can you handle criticism objectively and remain unmoved under it?

20. Do you retain control of yourself when things go wrong?

—R.E. Thompson, *Spiritual Leadership*

My attitude determines how I see…

MYSELF	—I cannot go any higher than my self-image.
OTHERS	—I cannot go any higher than my belief in others.
BUSINESS	—I cannot go any higher than my dream for my career.
MY FAILURES	—I cannot go any higher than my willingness to get back up.

The major difference between achieving people and average people is their _____ PERCEPTION _____

of and _____ RESPONSE _____ to failure.

—John Maxwell, *Failing Forward*

 **consider THIS**

Robert Half International, a San Francisco consulting firm, asked vice presidents and personnel directors at one hundred of America's largest companies to name the single greatest reason for firing an employee. While incompetence ranked as the number one reason, the next five reasons all involved *attitude*. (You can read more about this on pages 98–99 in *Developing the Leader Within You* by John Maxwell.)

A negative attitude never advances a leader's influence, and certainly will not attract more people of a higher caliber to you.

For some, a positive attitude comes more naturally than for others, but for all who desire to lead with success, a positive attitude is a must. A positive attitude displays itself in many forms—from faith in people to seeing the best in a difficult situation.

A positive attitude does not mean that you reject reality. It does mean, however, that if you commit yourself to it, you can find the best, even in the worst of situations. This will help you turn a negative situation into a positive one. A positive attitude is like a pair of glasses that focuses on the opportunities and possibilities in life, even in difficult times.

What kind of attitude glasses do you wear? Do you need a new set to give you better attitude vision?

Paradoxical Commandments of Leadership

1. People are illogical, unreasonable and self-centered.

   Love them anyway.

2. If you do good, people will accuse you of selfish, ulterior motives.

   Do good anyway.

3. If you are successful, you win false friends and true enemies.

   Succeed anyway.

4. The good you do today will be forgotten tomorrow.

   Do good anyway.

5. Honesty and frankness make you vulnerable.

   Be honest and frank anyway.

6. The biggest men with the biggest ideas can be shot down by the smallest men with the smallest minds.

   Think big anyway.

7. People favor underdogs but follow only top dogs.

   Fight for a few underdogs anyway.

8. What you spend years building may be destroyed overnight.

   Build anyway.

9. People really need help, but may attack you if you do help them.

   Help them anyway.

10. Give the world the best you have and you'll get kicked in the teeth.

    Give the world the best you have anyway.

 Remember: work hard, work smart, and most importantly, work in such a way that you produce results that make a difference. Don't let small thinking, complainers or self-centered folks undermine your leadership. Press on.

STOP *and Assess*

These questions will help you evaluate yourself further:

1. Name things other people do that discourage you in your leadership role.

2. Even when your motives are right, are you afraid of someone seeing you as insincere or self-centered?

3. Do you tend to overlook the underdogs?

4. Do you hold back your best for fear it will be trampled upon and unappreciated?

Practical Guidelines:

The following practical guidelines will help you increase your confidence in leadership:

- Instead of seeing negative, unreasonable people, see what they can become. Invest time in these people and love them.

- View obstacles as opportunities for success. Your confidence to lead will be stretched as you meet obstacles.

Bury a person in the snows of Valley Forge, and you have a George Washington. Raise him in abject poverty, and you have an Abraham Lincoln. Strike him down with infantile paralysis, and he becomes a Franklin D. Roosevelt. Have him or her born black in a society filled with racial discrimination, and you have a Booker T. Washington, a Marian Anderson, a George Washington Carver or a Martin Luther King, Jr. Call him a slow learner and retarded—writing him off as uneducable, and you have an Albert Einstein.

Remember...

Your attitude is not based on where you live or where you were born. It is based on your freedom to choose. The attitude you have is the one you choose!

Lesson One

What is a Leader?

Part Two Overview

Introduce the Lesson   *(5 minutes)*

Again, you are focusing on the basic principles of leadership in this lesson. Allow the class to briefly share what they learned after completing their exercises from the last lesson.

This lesson will explain three more characteristics of a leader: A leader is a dreamer, excellent in all he/she does and relational. This is a crucial lesson on casting vision, setting standards and valuing people.

Watch the Lesson   *(25–35 minutes)*

Make sure everyone is comfortable and can see the screen easily; then show the video.

Group Discussion   *(15 minutes)*

1. Ask for one practical way that each person can implement the "Rebekah principle."

2. Ask participants to mentally visualize themselves with a member of their organization who is often negative and self-absorbed. Encourage participants to think of at least two ways in which they can positively motivate this negative person.

    Ask several volunteers to share their solutions.

3. Ask everyone to share ideas they have found to be effective to build up and encourage other people.

4. As a group, brainstorm simple ideas for connecting with people.

Challenge   *(5 minutes)*

Ask each group member to set aside at least a half hour that week to complete the **Stop and Assess** exercises.

Also, ask them to spend time reflecting on how they can practically apply the principles they learned from Lesson One (parts one and two) to their daily leadership trials.

Lesson One

What is a Leader?

Part Two

When I see a **LEADER**, *I think of the word…*

LEADERSHIP

EQUIPPER

ATTITUDE

D REAMER _____

E

R

~

We all live under the same sky, but we don't all have the same horizon.

—Konrad Adenauer

~

There are four vision-levels of people:

1. Some people never see it (_____ WANDERER _____).

   These people wander through life.

2. Some people see it but never pursue it on their own (_____ FOLLOWER _____).

   These people will follow you but will only do it if you do it.

3. Some people see it and pursue it (_____ ACHIEVER _____).

   These are the people who don't need anyone else to help them. They'll do it.

4. Some people see it and pursue it and help others see it (_____ LEADER _____).

   These are the people who take others with them on the trip.

Vision Weaves Four Things Into the Fabric of our Daily Lives

1. _____ PASSION _____ —There is no such thing as an emotionless vision.

2. _____ MOTIVATION _____ —A vision is a picture of the future that motivates you to pursue it.

3. _____ DIRECTION _____ —A vision will prioritize your life.

4. _____ PURPOSE _____ —A vision makes you an important link between current reality and the future.

—Andy Stanley, *Visioneering*

A person without experience sees a vision idealistically. To that individual the vision alone is enough. Naively, this person casts the vision to others, expecting the dream to do the work and failing to realize that a vision needs support. A person with experience learns that people buy into the leader *before* they buy into the vision. Experienced leaders realize that people are fickle and dreams are fragile. Experience has taught me these principles about vision.

- The credibility of a vision is determined by the _____ LEADER _____ .

- The acceptance of a vision is determined by the _____ TIMING _____ of its presentation.

- The value of a vision is determined by the _____ ENERGY AND DIRECTION _____ it gives.

- The evaluation of a vision is determined by the _____ COMMITMENT _____ level of people.

- The success of a vision is determined by its _____ OWNERSHIP _____ by both the leader and the people.

—John C. Maxwell, *Developing the Leader Within You*

~

What would be worse than being born blind?
She replied, *To have sight without vision.*

—Helen Keller

~

Break the Dream Down So Everyone Can...

1. _____ UNDERSTAND _____

2. _____ OWN _____

3. _____ CONTRIBUTE _____

4. _____ PASS IT OWN _____

A leader's vision is worthless unless the people buy into the leader first. People see the messenger before they hear the message. So think carefully about how you present yourself. Don't assume that your grand ideas will win the masses if you are not genuine in caring for others and are not credible.

 *and Assess*

Check your understanding and see if you are a hindrance to your vision.

1. Are you a limited leader? If so, you'll either lack the vision or the ability to successfully pass it on.

2. Are you a concrete thinker? This person will "lock in" to what *is* rather than what *can be*. Think outside of the box.

3. Are you a dogmatic talker? Most of the time, the dogmatist knows nothing but conventionally says something. For example, Tris Speaker, a baseball great, said in 1921, "[Babe] Ruth made a big mistake when he gave up pitching."

4. Do you see yourself as a continual loser? Past failures often generate a fear of risking and pursuing a vision. Put failures behind you and view each new venture as another opportunity for success.

5. Are you satisfied with the status quo? Once you've achieved a comfort zone, are you satisfied to just sit and roll with complacency, predictability and even boredom?

6. Are you a tradition lover? Do you continue in a rut simply because "That's the way we've always done it"?

7. Do you feel safer if you stick with the majority? True leaders are always in the minority because they are thinking ahead of the present majority.

8. Do you see a problem in every solution? Seeing problems is not a hallmark of a mature person. It's generally the mark of a person without maturity and real vision to press on toward the goal.

9. Do you live ultimately for self? People who live for themselves are in a mighty small business. They don't accomplish much and are vision-busters.

10. Do you forecast failure and pessimism? These people predict doom and gloom. Times are always bad and money is always tight.

Are you surprised at some of your answers? Read through the questions again, this time answering them the way you want and need to be as a leader.

*When I see a **LEADER**, I think of the word…*

LEADERSHIP

EQUIPPER

ATTITUDE

DREAMER

E XCELLENCE _____

R

Excellence derives from the word "excel," which means to go _____ BEYOND AVERAGE _____ .

~

Don't be afraid to give your best to what seemingly are small jobs.
Every time you conquer one it makes you that much stronger.
If you do little jobs well, the big ones tend to take care of themselves.

—Dale Carnegie

~

Today's philosophy—Minimum _____ EFFORT _____ for maximum _____ EXPECTATION _____

Rebekah principle—Maximum _____ EFFORT _____ for minimum _____ EXPECTATION _____

Rebekah teaches us that…

(1.) We are not to live our lives as a _____ LEGALIST _____ .

(2.) We cannot walk the second mile until we have walked the _____ FIRST _____ .

(3.) Extra blessings are a result of extra _____ EFFORT _____ .

~

There is no traffic jam on the extra mile.

—Zig Ziglar

~

 Read the following standards. Is your leadership characterized by these statements? These principles can help you stay focused on going the extra mile and upholding your integrity in order to excel.

1. I will live what I teach.

2. I will do what I say.

3. I will be honest with others.

4. I will put what is best for others ahead of what is best for me.

5. I will be transparent and vulnerable.

Remember...

There are two paths that people can take in life. They can either play now and pay later, or pay now and play later. Regardless of the choice you make, one thing is certain: Life will demand a payment.

Doing my best at this present moment puts me in the best place for the next moment.

—Oprah Winfrey

Leaders never make decisions based on personal gain. Excellent leaders do it because it's right—not because they gain.

 **and Assess**

These are important questions that will show you the inner feelings with which you lead:

1. Can you truly say that you make leadership decisions so that all involved benefit?

2. How often do you go the extra mile—and when you do, with what expectations?

After answering these questions, what needs to change in your thinking about going the extra mile and your expectations?

When I see a **LEADER**, *I think of the word…*

LEADERSHIP

EQUIPPER

ATTITUDE

DREAMER

EXCELLENCE

R ELATIONSHIPS _____

You can't lead'em if you don't lov'em!

Why Customers Quit

___1%___ % Die

___3%___ % Move away

___5%___ % Other friendships

___9%___ % Competition

___14%___ % Product dissatisfaction

___68%___ % Attitude of indifference toward the customer

You may have heard it said that people do not care how much you know until they know how much you care. Successful teachers, writers, managers, politicians, philosophers and leaders who deal with people instinctively know this simple fact: Every person in the world is hungry for something, be it recognition, companionship, understanding, love—the list is endless. One common item on people's list of needs is the desire to feel worthwhile. As a leader, you can develop solid relationships by helping a person become useful and find satisfaction and significance.

Napoleon Bonaparte knew every officer of his army by name. He liked to wander through his camp, meet an officer, greet him by name, and talk about a battle or maneuver he knew this officer had been involved in. He never missed an opportunity to inquire about a soldier's hometown, wife and family; the men were always amazed to see how much detailed personal information about each one the emperor was able to store in his memory.

Since every officer felt Napoleon's personal interest in him—proven by his statements and questions—it's easy to understand the devotion they felt for him.

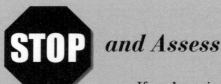

STOP *and Assess*

If you're going to lead them, you have to love them. Loving them and leading them go hand in hand. Meaningful relationships are real relationships.

The following questions will help you reflect on your own ability to establish meaningful relationships as a leader.

Think of people you have spent at least thirty minutes with this week…

1. Did you initiate the time or did they?

2. Were the meetings for the purpose of relationships, counseling, communication or development?

3. Do you seek to impress people by keeping a distance or do you try to impact them by getting to know them personally?

An old Chinese poem has some of the best advice you can find about developing relationships.

Go to the people,
Live among them.
Learn from them.
Love them.
Start with what they know,
Build on what they have.
But of the best leaders,
When their task is accomplished,
Their work is done,
The people will remark,
"We have done it ourselves."

 **and Assess**

Think about your teachers. Which ones did you especially like? Most likely, they were the ones with whom you connected. The ability to connect and bond is crucial to effective leadership.

Your relationship with people is key to leading.

We build strong relationships through personal involvement. Check yourself on the following.

1. Do you allow yourself to look at situations and circumstances through the eyes of others?

2. Do you genuinely care for people before you try to develop them?

3. Do you look for opportunities to build up people?

4. Do you show favoritism to certain individuals or groups?

5. Do you emphasize the importance of the individual by asking for the opinions of others?

6. Do you seek to correct problems in private with a win-win approach?

consider THIS

People know if you love and believe in them. They can sense if you are in the relationship for their best interest or yours. Whether the relationship is brief or long-term, people have an inner sense about your motive. Sometimes they verbalize it in this way… "I do not know, I just have a good feeling about him."

In long-term relationships, it is easier for people to know if you love and believe in them, because your actions tell the truth every time.

Remember these three goals to help you connect in communication:

1. Give them something to feel.

2. Give them something to learn.

3. Give them something to hold on to.

The connection you make may be as simple as an encouraging word over a cup of coffee, but the connection is made.

Take This Quiz!

PROFILE OF A LEADER

Circle the appropriate answer

Key: 0 = Never 1 = Seldom 2 = Sometimes 3 = Usually 4 = Always

1.	They have influence.	0 1 2 3 4
2.	They have self-discipline.	0 1 2 3 4
3.	They have a good track record.	0 1 2 3 4
4.	They have strong people skills.	0 1 2 3 4
5.	They have the ability to solve problems.	0 1 2 3 4
6.	They do not accept the status quo.	0 1 2 3 4
7.	They see the big picture.	0 1 2 3 4
8.	They have the ability to handle stress.	0 1 2 3 4
9.	They display a positive spirit.	0 1 2 3 4
10.	They understand people.	0 1 2 3 4
11.	They are free of personal problems.	0 1 2 3 4
12.	They are willing to take responsibility.	0 1 2 3 4
13.	They are free from anger.	0 1 2 3 4
14.	They are willing to make changes.	0 1 2 3 4
15.	They have integrity.	0 1 2 3 4
16.	They have a growing personal walk with God.	0 1 2 3 4
17.	They have the ability to see what needs to be done next.	0 1 2 3 4
18.	People follow their leadership.	0 1 2 3 4
19.	They have the ability and desire to keep on learning.	0 1 2 3 4
20.	They have a manner which draws people.	0 1 2 3 4
21.	They have a good self-image.	0 1 2 3 4
22.	They have a willingness to submit to and serve others.	0 1 2 3 4
23.	They have the ability to "bounce back" when problems arise.	0 1 2 3 4
24.	They have the ability to develop other leaders.	0 1 2 3 4
25.	They take initiative.	0 1 2 3 4

Total Points

Lesson Two

Leadership is Influence

Part One Overview

Introduce the Lesson *(5 minutes)*

Open up by sharing what you learned and asking what everyone else learned from doing their **Stop and Assess** exercises from last week.

This lesson will communicate one central theme clearly: *Leadership is influence. Nothing more, nothing less.* This principle is key to having the right perspective on what it takes to become a strong leader.

For your members who are not naturally gifted as leaders, this lesson will be a breakthrough lesson for them. They will learn practical ways to become the leaders they aspire to be.

Watch the Lesson *(25–35 minutes)*

Make sure everyone is comfortable and can see the screen easily; then show the video.

Group Discussion *(15 minutes)*

1. Ask participants, "Have you ever tried to lead by declaring your title and expecting people to automatically follow? What happened?" Have several people share their answers.

2. Demonstrating that you care is a vital part of influencing others. Ask several volunteers to suggest ways to show they care for people in a working relationship. Take these suggestions and put them into practical scenarios. Keep this simple.

3. Ask volunteers to share a tough leadership experience in which they were called upon to make an unpopular but necessary decision. How did others in the organization respond?

Challenge *(5 minutes)*

Ask each group member to set aside at least a half hour that week to complete the **Stop and Assess** exercises.

Remind them to each take time to honestly evaluate how well they get along with other people. Are they nurturing and encouraging? Or are they hard and discouraging?

Make sure everyone is reading the *Developing the Leader Within You* book!

Lesson Two

Leadership is Influence

Part One

Influence Insights:

1. Leadership is _____INFLUENCE_____ . Nothing more, nothing less.

The very essence of all power to influence lies in getting the other person to participate.

—Harry A. Overstreet

The person who has the most influence is the leader.

A Leader's Prayer

God, when I am wrong, make me willing to change.
When I am right, make me easy to live with.
So strengthen me that the power of my example
Will far exceed the authority of my rank.

—Pauline H. Peters

 **and Assess**

You can learn to influence in whatever area you lead or desire to lead. Remember that leadership is an art, not a science, and it is a process, not an event, so you can increase your influence if you will take the following steps.

1. Why do you want to be a leader?

2. Are you willing to pay the price?

3. What do you hope the results and rewards of leadership will be?

4. Is anyone following your leadership?

5. Are the right people responding to your leadership?

6. If you did not give them a paycheck, would you still have influence?

7. Would people follow your lead if you did not have your title?

If you need improvement in the above areas, consider the following to increase your influence:

Develop your passion for people and relationship skills. How? The above questions point you directly toward those things that will develop your skills.

2. Our influence with others usually is not in _____ALL AREAS_____ .

Anytime you think you have influence, try ordering around someone else's dog.

—The Cockle Burr

A Born Leader

I'm paid to be a foreman.
My job is leading men.
My boss thinks I'm a natural,
But if I am, why then,
I wish someone would tell me
Why snow-swept walks I clean,
When in the house sit two grown sons
Who made the football team.

—Author Unknown

We don't influence people in all areas. If your knowledge of computers is limited, people won't look to you for influence in this area.

A leader must care...

You don't have to be an expert in all things. Remember that people will follow you when they know you care and are committed to them.

Trust is a key ingredient if you are to show people you care. Trust is a lifestyle that over the long haul reveals the true value of uncompromised character.

Using the following 10 hallmarks of character that build trust in relationships, rate yourself on the scale of 1–10: 1=poor; 10=strong. Have someone else rate you also.

1. Honesty Score: _____

This is not simply the absence of lying, but a commitment to tell the truth. Honesty is one of the many non-negotiable virtues of your character that produces trust.

2. Discipline Score: _____

Self-control is the key element of discipline. If we do not have self-control in the small things of life, we do not have self-control in the larger, more important things of life. To influence others and develop sincere relationships, trust is essential.

3. Humility Score: _____

Arrogance never wins anyone to your side. Pride pushes people away from you and an independent attitude burns bridges that ultimately destroys the relationships you wish to build.

4. Good Motives Score: _____

Good motives are about doing your dead level best to put the best interests of others before your own interests and desires. It is about your honest and sincere intent, not a flawless life.

5. Integrity Score: _____

Integrity is doing what you say you will do. It is doing the right thing even when no one else is watching. Integrity is an absolute must in showing others you care.

6. Courage Score: _____

Plainly put, if a leader is fearful, the people will be concerned that, under pressure, he or she will compromise their security by selling out on core values and convictions. Courage demonstrated by a leader weaves strength and trust into relationships.

7. Work Ethic Score: _____

Leadership is not about perks, privileges and recognition. It is about responsibility and results. If the people you are responsible for believe they work harder than you do, or that you do not put forth passionate effort, trust will begin to deteriorate. The people will believe that your concern for them is minimal, at best, and perhaps nonexistent.

8. Compassion Score: _____

People do not care about how good you are unless they believe it will benefit them in some way. A leader must demonstrate care and compassion to his/her organization if true relationships are to be built.

9. Commitment Score: _____

The people in your organization will never be more committed than you are. Your personal commitment is the bar for their commitment. You must be committed to show that you care.

10. Consistency Score: _____

This is a core component of trust. Erratic behavior breaks down trust. Mood swings, lack of continuity, emotional outbursts and unpredictable professional and personal behavior patterns destroy relationships. Your character will be in question and your leadership will suffer greatly.

Well, how did you do? Remember, this is not about perfection, but progress in developing relationships with others.

People must know that you care in order to trust you. Your influence as a leader will only go as far as the relationships you build through genuine concern for others.

3. With influence comes _____RESPONSIBILITY_____ .

There are people whose feelings and well-being are within my influence.
I will never escape that fact.

—John Maxwell

 **STOP** *and Assess*

How can you be a responsible leader? Demonstrate that you care and are willing to go the extra mile, and you'll find that your influence as a leader will increase. Here are some practical ways to show others you care:

- Learn people's names quickly.

- Be more interested in making people feel good about themselves than in making people feel good about you.

- Smile often and keep a positive attitude.

- Be a good listener. Ask the other person questions in order to learn more about him or her.

Copy the above points onto an index card and tuck it in your desk drawer, your briefcase or place it on your desk. These things will remind you of characteristics that are essential if you aspire to be a responsible leader.

4. My influence with others is either _____POSITIVE_____ or _____NEGATIVE_____ .

My Influence

My life shall touch a dozen lives before this day is done,
Leave countless marks for good or ill ere sets the evening sun,
This is the wish I always wish, the prayer I always pray;
God, may my life help other lives it touches by the way.

—Author Unknown

 **STOP** *and Assess*

As a leader, you will either help people or hurt them. And your influence reaches far! Sociologists tell us that even the most introverted individual will influence ten thousand other people during his or her lifetime. (You can read more about how far-reaching your influence is on pages 2–4 in *Developing the Leader Within You* by John Maxwell.)

Ask yourself, do others desire to be around me or do they avoid me?

The answer reveals much about whether you are helping or hurting others.

5. People of positive influence _____ADD VALUE_____ to others.

A life isn't significant except for its impact upon our lives.

—Jackie Robinson

Success is when I add value to _____MYSELF_____ .

Significance is when I add value to _____OTHERS_____ .

STOP *and Assess*

In what way does your leadership role add value to others? The following questions will help you determine this.

1. Does my work play to my strengths or the strengths of others?

2. Do I recognize the success of others?

3. Do I have an "extra-mile-whatever-it-takes attitude"?

4. Am I interested in earning credit or do I willingly share it with others?

To create a climate or environment where others are esteemed is essential to develop and strengthen your leadership. This climate will also provide the necessary atmosphere for everyone in the organization, or your department, to grow and succeed in fulfilling their responsibilities.

Influencing others is a choice.

You make the choice about how you will influence others. Don't wait for them to come to you. The litmus test of whether or not you are an encouraging leader is if people migrate to you at times other than when they need something from you. Simply put, do people seek you out? Check the following:

1. Do people seek you out, not for permission or a signature, but to be around you?

2. When you see people—before work, after work, at lunch, at church— do they smile and walk toward you or do they continue on their path?

These are important observations for you to make.

10 Ways That An Influencer Gains Influence

An Influencer has...

1. **I**NTEGRITY _____ with people

If we live truly, we shall truly live.

—Ralph Waldo Emerson

In order to be a leader a man must have followers. And to have followers,
a man must have their confidence. Hence the supreme quality for a leader is,
unquestionably, integrity. Without it, no real success is possible, no matter
whether it is on a section gang, a football field, in an army or in an office.
If a man's associates find him guilty of phoniness, if they find that he lacks forthright
integrity, he will fail. His teachings and actions must square with each other.
The first great need, therefore, is integrity and high purpose.

—Dwight D. Eisenhower

 In the business world it's acceptable to make mistakes, to lay eggs—big ones—but the Center for Creative Research, in a significant study, learned that one thing that sounds the death knell for those who aspire to the top rung on the ladder is betraying a trust. Virtually anything else can be overcome over a period of time, but once trust is betrayed, moving to the top of the ladder is out of the question.

Few men have virtue to withstand the highest bidder.

—George Washington

An example of integrity in action:

Some years earlier in Johnson & Johnson's mission statement they had a line saying that "They would operate with honesty and integrity." Several weeks before the Tylenol incident, the president of Johnson & Johnson sent a memo to all presidents of divisions of Johnson & Johnson asking if they were abiding by, and if they believed in, the mission statement. All presidents came back in the affirmative.

The story goes that within an hour of the Tylenol crisis, the president of Tylenol ordered all capsules off the shelf—knowing it was a $100 million dollar decision.

When reporters asked how he could decide so easily and rapidly on such a major decision, his reply was, "I was practicing what we agreed on in our mission statement." It is always easy to do right when you know ahead of time what you stand for.

The man who has no inner life is the slave of his surroundings.
—Henri Frédéric Amiel

Abraham Lincoln said, *When I lay down the reins of this administration I want to have one friend left. And that friend is inside myself.*

Notre Dame football coach, Lou Holtz, in a motivational film said:
Do what's right! Do the best you can and treat others the way you want to be treated because they will ask three questions:

1) *Can I trust you?*

2) *Do you believe this? Are you committed to this? Have a passion for this?*

3) *Do you care about me as a person?*

Integrity is not what we do so much as who we are. The more credible you are the more confidence people place in you.

STOP *and Assess*

Your answers to the following questions will determine if you are into image-building instead of integrity-building:

1. Are you the same person regardless of who you are with? Yes or No

2. Do you make decisions that are best for others when another choice would benefit you? Yes or No

3. Are you quick to recognize others for their efforts and contributions to your success? Yes or No

If you answered "No" to even one of these questions, stop here and ask yourself what you need to do to change that answer to a "Yes."

Thomas Macauley said, *The measure of a man's real character is what he would do if he would never be found out.* Does that quote describe you?

Integrity will not allow our lips to violate our hearts. There will be no discrepancy between what we appear to be and what our family knows we are, whether in times of prosperity or adversity.

If what I say and do are not the same, the results are inconsistent.

Do you...

Say to the employees, "Be at work on time," yet you arrive late?

Say to the employees, "Be positive," yet you complain and exhibit a negative attitude?

Say to the employees, "Put the customer first," yet put yourself first?

A leader with double standards will have little influence!

An Influencer...

2. **N** <u>URTURES</u> people

The length and breadth of our influence upon others depends on the depth of our concern for others.

Many leaders love their position more than their people.

When that happens, leaders soon lose their <u>POSITION</u> .

Of course it is possible to love a human being, if you don't know them too long.

—Charles Bukowski

My parents have been visiting me for a few days.
I just dropped them off at the airport.
They leave tomorrow.

—Margaret Smith

When Narvaez, the Spanish patriot, lay dying, his father-confessor asked him *whether he had forgiven all his enemies.* Narvaez looked astonished and said, "Father, I have no enemies. I have shot them all."

 Few leaders love their people more than their position.

When that happens, leaders _____STRENGTHEN_____ their position.

Achievers Care About People

"Nice guys" get the best results from subordinates, according to a study by the research outfit Telometrics International, as reported in the *Wall Street Journal.* Of 16,000 executives studied, the 13 percent identified as "high achievers" tended to care about people as well as profits. Average achievers concentrated on production, while low achievers were preoccupied with their own security.

High achievers viewed subordinates optimistically, while low achievers showed a basic distrust of subordinates' abilities. High achievers sought advice from their subordinates; low achievers didn't. High achievers were listeners; moderate achievers listened only to superiors; low achievers avoided communication and relied on policy manuals.

—*Wall Street Journal*

Notes on Nurturing:

A. Nurturing people does not mean _____NEEDING_____ people.

You can't lead people if you need people.

—John Maxwell

 **and Assess**

Do you have to have the approval of other people? If so, you'll never be able to make the hard decisions.

B. Nurturing people does mean you will make a _____COMMITMENT_____ to people.

Love will find a way. Indifference will find an excuse.

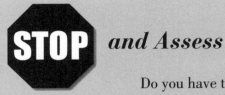 **and Assess**

Are you committed to lead people regardless of difficulty?

Do you have a genuine love for people to work through the hard times and lead them through the valleys?

These are critical elements in leadership.

C. Nurturing people does mean _____LOVING_____ people.

You will find as you look back upon your life that the moments when you have really lived, are the moments when you have done things in a spirit of love.

—Henry Drummond

D. Nurturing people does mean _____LIFTING_____ people to a higher level.

Jan Carlzon, chairman and CEO of Scandinavian Airlines, speaks from his experience when he suggests that there are two great motivators in life. One is fear. The other is love. You can lead an organization by fear, but if you do, you will ensure that people won't perform up to their real capabilities.

Deep down, your players must know you care about them.
This is the most important thing. I could never get away with what I do if
the players felt I didn't care. They know, in the long run, I'm in their corner.

—Bo Schembechler, former head football coach, University of Michigan

 **STOP** *and Assess*

As a leader, you are somewhat of a caretaker. You must be able to nurture others. Leaders have such a healthy care and respect for people that they never abuse them or misuse them.

1. What's your attitude about people? You can't nurture someone whom you perceive as a resource.

2. Do you seek to exalt and praise others?

Remember: you can lead for a lifetime if people know you care about them as individuals.

An Influencer has...

3. **F**AITH_____ in people

Every man is entitled to be valued by his best moments.

—Ralph Waldo Emerson

_____ASSETS_____ make things possible.

_____PEOPLE_____ make things happen.

In leading others, there are three feelings that a leader cannot possess:

(1) _____FEAR_____

(2) _____DISLIKE_____

(3) _____CONTEMPT_____

If we are afraid of people we cannot _____HANDLE_____ them.

If we dislike people we should not _____LEAD_____ them.

If we look down on people we will not _____RESPECT_____ them.

 **and Assess**

Leadership is hindered without faith in people. Check yourself on the following:

1. Do you openly acknowledge your confidence in others?

2. Do you work to rid yourself of any dislike for particular individuals?

3. Do you see yourself as elevated above others, intellectually, through position or otherwise?

Others will know if you have confidence and faith in them. Work to maintain a belief in the people in your organization.

Les Giblin, an authority on human relations, says that our actions must be genuine: You can't make the other fellow feel important in your presence if you secretly feel that he is a nobody.

Give your key leaders a reputation to uphold.

You can show people that you believe in them through:

- Love for them

    This strengthens personal relationships.

- Believing in them

    This will give them courage to stretch themselves and take risks.

- Getting to know them

    This strengthens a person's individual growth.

- Teaching them

    This enhances growth.

- Expanding them

    This will provide challenges.

- Lifting them

    This will ensure results.

Lesson Two

Leadership is Influence

Part Two Overview

Introduce the Lesson   *(5 minutes)*

Open up by sharing what you learned and asking what everyone else learned from doing their **Stop and Assess** exercises from last week.

This lesson will continue to communicate the theme that leadership is influence. This part of the lesson covers how to listen, understand, navigate, connect, empower, and reproduce oneself in other potential leaders.

This lesson is highly practical and applicable—make sure that everyone is taking notes as they listen to what they can be applying immediately in their lives.

Watch the Lesson   *(25–35 minutes)*

Make sure everyone is comfortable and can see the screen easily; then show the video.

Group Discussion   *(15 minutes)*

1. Refer to the listening quiz. Ask for volunteers who will share the results. Ask participants to suggest practical tips for better listening.

2. Ask which of the five reasons that all leaders don't reproduce other leaders (listed on page 53) most applies to them.

3. Ask team members to practice connecting with others. Have them divide into groups of two for 5–7 minutes. Then return as a group and ask volunteers to share what they learned as they deliberately tried to connect.

Challenge   *(5 minutes)*

Ask each group member to set aside at least a half hour that week to complete the **Stop and Assess** exercises.

Have everyone ask two people that they are especially close to how they rate on each of the 10 marks of an influencer.

Lesson Two

Leadership is Influence

Part Two

An Influencer...

4. L<u>ISTENS</u>_____ to people.

Climbing the "Ladder" to Better Listening

L stands for: _____LOOK_____ at the speaker.

Meanings are not in words but in people.

A stands for: _____ASK_____ questions.

This is the quickest way to become a listener.

D stands for: _____DON'T_____ interrupt.

It's just as rude to step on people's ideas as it is to step on their toes.

D stands for: _____DON'T_____ change the subject.

Listening is wanting to hear.

E stands for: Check your _____EMOTIONS_____ .

Leaders must keep "current of the undercurrents." Emotions create a storm and others will back away.

R stands for: _____RESPONSIVE_____ listening.

When people feel that their leader no longer listens or responds, they will go somewhere else.

The first duty of love is to listen.

—Paul Tillich

A wise old owl sat in an oak,
The more he heard the less he spoke.
The less he spoke the more he heard,
Why can't we be like that wise old bird?

—Author Unknown

Stop Stealing Ego Food

I'm willing to bet that everyone of you today, several times in fact, stole someone's "ego food"— the satisfaction their esteem needs.

You probably stole it and didn't even know it. For example, someone says, "I've really had a busy day," and you reply, "You've been busy! You should see all the work that has piled up on my desk for weeks and I can't even get to it."

What are you doing? You are taking away, you are stealing the very food, the satisfaction this person needs for his ego, his "I." In effect you are saying, "You may think that you're pretty good, but you're just average when it comes to being able to measure up."

Sam Walton, founder of Wal-Mart who became one of the richest men in America, believed in hearing what people—especially his employees—had to say. Once he flew his aircraft to Mt. Pleasant, Texas, and parked the plane with instructions to his co-pilot to meet him one hundred or so miles down the road. He then flagged a Wal-Mart truck and rode the rest of the way to "chat with the driver." He said, "It seemed like so much fun." It was also a great learning experience.

Dallas-based Chili's, one of the nation's five best-run food service chains, according to *Restaurants & Institutions* magazine, is another company with a leader who listens to employees. Norman Brinker, Chili's chairman, believes that responsive communication is the key to good relations with both employees and customers. He also has learned that such communication pays big dividends. Almost 80 percent of Chili's menu came from suggestions made by unit managers.

Listening is the way to gain wisdom because everything you say you already know.

 **and Assess**

The following test is useful to determine if you listen to people with more than your ears. Do you hear more than their words?

For the following questions, give yourself four points for answering *Always,* three points for *Usually,* two for *Rarely,* and one for *Never.*

Do I allow the speaker to finish without interrupting?　　　　　＿＿＿＿＿＿

Do I listen "between the lines," that is, for the subtext?　　　＿＿＿＿＿＿

When writing a message, do I listen for and write down
the key facts and phrases?　　　　　　　　　　　　　　　＿＿＿＿＿＿

Do I repeat what the person just said to clarify
the meaning?　　　　　　　　　　　　　　　　　　　　＿＿＿＿＿＿

Do I avoid getting hostile and/or agitated when I
disagree with the speaker?　　　　　　　　　　　　　　＿＿＿＿＿＿

Do I tune out distractions when listening?　　　　　　　　＿＿＿＿＿＿

Do I make an effort to seem interested in what the
other person is saying?　　　　　　　　　　　　　　　　＿＿＿＿＿＿

Scoring:

26 or higher: You are an excellent listener.

22–25: Better than average score.

18–21: Room for improvement.

17 or lower: Get out there right away and practice your listening.[1]

David Burns, a medical doctor and professor of psychiatry at the University of Pennsylvania, says: "The biggest mistake you can make in trying to talk convincingly is to put your highest priority on expressing your ideas and feelings. What most people really want is to be listened to, respected, and understood. The moment people see that they are being understood, they become more motivated to understand your point of view."

Practice, practice, practice true listening!

[1]Stephen Ash, "The Career Doctor," cited in Michigan Department of Social Services, *No-Name Newsletter,* Fall 1986.

An Influencer...

5. **U**NDERSTANDS _____ people.

Few things will pay you bigger dividends than the time and trouble you take to understand people. Almost nothing will add more to your stature as an executive and as a person. Nothing will give you greater satisfaction or bring you more happiness.

—Kienzle & Dare, *Climbing the Executive Ladder*

To understand the mind of a person look at what he/she has _____ ALREADY ACHIEVED _____ .

To understand the heart of a person look at what he/she _____ DREAMS OF BECOMING _____ .

Three Questions to Connect With Others

1. _____ WHAT DO YOU LAUGH ABOUT? _____

2. _____ WHAT DO YOU CRY ABOUT? _____

3. _____ WHAT DO YOU DREAM ABOUT? _____

Norman Wright says...

There are two basic reasons why relationships fail:

(1) _____ FEAR _____ , which causes us to erect barriers; and

(2) _____ SELFISHNESS _____ , which causes us to focus on self instead of others.

Wear muddy boots.

—Kansas Agricultural Advertising Agency's New Business Philosophy

At the beginning of the meeting the head of the agency reaches under the table and brings out a pair of muddy boots and puts them in the center of the conference room table. *Now folks,* he says, *this is our business philosophy at this agency: If you hire us, we will get our boots muddy. We will walk your fields with you. We will get as deeply involved in your business as you are. And we will thoroughly understand your problems before we try to create advertising solutions for you.*

 **and Assess**

There are at least three vital qualities that enable us to develop lasting relationships with understanding people. Ask yourself the following to see if you possess these characteristics:

1. Are you genuine in your concern for others? Do you operate behind a façade or the truth?

2. Do you accept people as they are?

3. Do you seek to understand the position of others?

4. Do you have empathy for other people?

People are the principal asset of any organization. Seek to understand them in order to provide solid and strong leadership.

Imagine that a person (volunteer or employee) in your organization speaks to you about serious conflicts in her life. She has major decisions to make that will affect her involvement in the organization. She is a valuable team player and asset to your group. What are your immediate thoughts?

Do your thoughts go something like this:

• How will this affect me?

• How will this affect my department/area of responsibility?

• Do you feel panic, frustration or anger at this person?

Understanding people means that while you may not understand the full picture, you seek to understand from their point of view. You desire to understand and you place understanding above immediate consequences. Your desire to understand will strengthen relationships, no matter the outcome.

Let's Review: How to Gain Influence

Integrity with people

Nurture people

Faith in people

Listen to people

Understand people

The first five steps = _____ATTITUDE_____

The last five steps = _____ACTION_____

An Influencer...

6. **E** NLARGES _____ people

Q. How do you grow an organization? _____GROW PEOPLE_____

Q. How do you grow people? _____GROW YOURSELF_____

~

There is no more noble occupation in the world than to assist another human being—
to help someone succeed.

—Alan Loy McGinnis

~

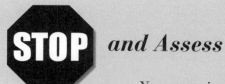 **STOP** *and Assess*

Your organization will not rise above your level.

Ask yourself the following:

1. Are you frustrated because your team has "peaked out" in growth?

2. If so, has your growth been significant to the point where others are growing also?

3. Is your agenda to enlarge, develop and grow others?

According to William J. H. Boetcker, people divide themselves into four classes. In which of these do you place yourself?

1. Those who always do less than they are told.

2. Those who will do what they are told, but nothing more.

3. Those who will do things without being told.

4. Those who will inspire others to do things.

Your responses should bring into clear view your attitude toward the growth of people.

Use the following to grow people:

1. Give credit for their suggestions.

2. Encourage them.

3. Don't criticize them in front of other people.

4. Ask others for their opinions.

5. Inform employees of their progress.

6. Don't play favorites.

Six Essentials to Enlarging Others

1. Placing a _____HIGH VALUE_____ on people

2. A personal commitment to _____GROWTH_____

3. A personal commitment to _____ADD VALUE TO OTHERS_____

4. The ability to communicate your _____BELIEF_____ in others

5. The ability to _____STRETCH_____ them

6. Your _____HIGHEST JOY_____ is other people's success

Success is...

<u>   KNOWING   </u> my purpose in life

<u>   GROWING   </u> to my maximum potential

<u>   SOWING   </u> seeds that benefit others

—John C. Maxwell, *The Success Journey*

 The first objective of a leader is to develop people, not dismiss them. Studies have shown that day-to-day coaching is most effective for growing people and seeing their most effective performance.

Give employees opportunities to grow. Give them responsibilities that show that you trust them. Provide learning opportunities through work experience, seminars, educational opportunities and mentoring relationships.

An Influencer...

7. **N** <u>AVIGATES   </u> for people

The Law of Navigation: Anyone can steer the ship, but it takes a leader to chart the course.

The man who goes alone can start the day.
But he who travels with another must wait until the other is ready.

—Henry David Thoreau

The leadership surveys of Warren Bennis and Burt Nanus spell it out in black and white: *What we have found is that the higher the rank, the more interpersonal and human the undertaking. Our top executives spend roughly 90 percent of their time concerned with the messiness of people problems.*

A leader is one who sees _____MORE_____ than others see.

A leader is one who sees _____FARTHER_____ than others see.

A leader is one who sees _____BEFORE_____ others see.

 **STOP** *and Assess*

A leader is one with a clear idea of where he or she is going. Do you have an itinerary? The following questions will help you determine if you're on course:

1. Do I have the end clearly in mind?

2. Do the other key personnel around me understand the desired results as clearly as I do?

3. Am I prepared to pay the price to achieve my objective?

4. Are those closest to me supportive of this endeavor?

Planning the Trip...

After you know where you're going, make sure you have the right tools.

1. Have I figured out how to achieve my goal (at least as far ahead as is reasonable to plan)? And written it down?

2. Have I considered the resources necessary?

3. Do I have the right people?

4. Have I written out a time line?

5. Have I anticipated the obstacles?

6. Have I sought wise counsel?

7. Do I personally possess the gifts and energy needed to achieve the objective?

A prepared traveler doesn't avoid all of the bumps in the road. But to look ahead and contemplate saves time and energy and gives you confidence as you proceed.

continued

STOP

continued

Navigation is a complicated process, but broken down into its key components it is easy to apply. Study these practical steps. They will help you accomplish your mission in your organization.

1. **Have a clear vision.** Pass out a 3 x 5 card to your top leaders and possibly everyone in your organization. Ask them to write on one side the overall goal or mission of the organization (or their department), and on the other side of the card ask them to write their key contribution to the achievement of that mission, goal, etc. Don't give study or "prep" time. Collect the cards in 5–7 minutes. To evaluate, check to see if they know the actual mission or goal of the organization. Who is responsible for that? You!

2. **Chart the course in detail.** Think through every facet of the project or mission. Regardless of the length of time you will need, think it through. The more preparation and planning, the greater the likelihood for success. Take the time to literally chart your course on paper. Update and change the plan as needed.

3. **Seek wise counsel.** Ask questions and study the work of others who have more experience and exposure than you. It's a waste of valuable time to re-invent the wheel and make mistakes that have already been made. List people with whom you can talk, observe and read about who can save you time as you pursue the goals of your organization.

Remember...

Even the most masterful and detailed plans must be occasionally modified over the course of time. The longer the time, the more corrections must be made. Be willing to alter and adjust your plan.

An Influencer...

8. **C** <u>ONNECTS</u> _____ with people

All great leaders and communicators have one thing in common:

They _____ CONNECT _____ with people.

Connecting thoughts:

(1) Connecting with people is the _____ LEADER'S _____ responsibility.

(2) Connecting with people means _____ CARING _____ for people.

(3) Connecting with people means _____ READING _____ people.

(4) Connecting with people means going to their agenda _____ FIRST _____ .

In 1842, Abraham Lincoln addressed members of the Washingtonian Temperance Society. In the address, entitled "Charity in Temperance Reform," Lincoln made this timeless observation,

> _If you would win a man to your cause, first convince him that you are his sincere friend...Assume to dictate to his judgment, or to command his action, or to mark him as one to be shunned and despised, and he will retreat within himself...you shall no more be able to pierce him, than to penetrate the hard shell of a tortoise with a rye straw._
>
> —Carl Sandburg, _The Prairie Years_

 **and Assess**

As you learn to connect with others, make it a habit to study the connection abilities of others. You will learn much through observation.

To evaluate your own connection skills, use the following questions to gain insight:

1. When you first meet people in a group or individually, does the conversation seem to flow easily?

2. When you are engaged in conversation, do you find and focus on the other person's agenda?

3. When you are speaking in public or in private conversation, do you seek common ground?

4. In dealing with people, both audiences and privately, are you open and honest or reserved and self-protected?

continued

STOP

continued

5. When you are addressing an audience, large or small, are you aware of the atmosphere and how people are perceiving the experience?

6. When you speak to an audience, are you focusing on the whole crowd or on individuals?

7. What are the key signals that tell you a connection has been made?

8. Was your time together more heart-to-heart or head-to-head?

Remember, if you cannot connect with people on a one-to-one basis, you will have great difficulty connecting with larger groups.

Now study and work on the following principles to improve your connection skills with people.

1. **Be real.** Just be yourself! Be open and candid about what you think and feel, and people will respond. It doesn't mean everyone likes or agrees with you, but they can connect with you.

2. **Exercise intimacy, trust and vulnerability in relationships.** If people cannot see your heart (intimacy), they cannot connect with you. If they cannot connect, they can't trust you—and if they can't trust you, they will not follow you.

3. **Find a way to identify with others.** Seek to find common ground with others.

4. **Don't use rank, power or authority to "make" others follow you.** This is not effective, and it certainly does not aid in helping people connect with you.

5. **Abandon feelings of superiority.** In most relationships, even ground is rare. One person is above the other in some respect, whether it is education, income or experience. Feelings of superiority are connection killers!

6. **Believe and expect the best in people.** Fight cynicism and distrust.

7. **Add value to the lives of others.** They will connect with you when they believe you esteem them. Do this through encouragement, teaching and/or coaching.

STOP

continued

Your checklist for evaluating if you have a good connection:

☐ The audience wants more.

☐ The person you are talking with seems relaxed and at ease.

☐ The audience is focused and engaged in the appropriate response (e.g., laughing, taking notes, etc.)

☐ There is a sense of warmth and inner fulfillment.

☐ You feel like you have identified with each other.

☐ You personally would enjoy repeating the experience.

☐ After the conversation is over, you both know something about each other you did not know before.

☐ After the exchange is over, you both have something of value added to your life.

☐ The time together had depth and meaning; it was not just a shallow exchange.

☐ You felt like the time together was more heart-to-heart than head-to-head.

Challenge...

Seek to make connections with someone who is difficult to connect with.

An Influencer...

9. **E** MPOWERS _____ people

The Law of Navigation: Anyone can steer the ship but it takes a leader to chart the course.

No matter how much work you can do, no matter how engaging your personality may be, you will not advance far in business if you cannot work through others.

—John Craig

Enlarging a person deals with their _____INDIVIDUAL_____ growth.

Empowering a person deals with their _____ORGANIZATIONAL_____ growth.

In 1924, an English artist by the name of William Wolcott came to New York City to record his impressions of that great metropolis. One morning he was visiting in the office of a former colleague when the urge to sketch came over him. Seeing some paper on his friend's desk, he asked, "May I have that?" His friend answered, "That's not sketching paper. That's ordinary wrapping paper." Not wanting to lose that spark of inspiration, Wolcott took the wrapping paper and said, "Nothing is ordinary if you know how to use it." On that ordinary wrapping paper, Wolcott made two sketches. In 1924, long before our inflated values, one of those sketches sold for five hundred dollars and the other sold for one thousand dollars. Ordinary wrapping paper in the hands of a great artist became a great masterpiece.

Empowerment Means...

Seeing the potential of an individual.

Saying encouraging, empowering words to that person.

Sharing your power and position and influence with them.

Showing to others your belief in and power given to that person.

The Five Essentials to Empowerment

(1) Find a person _____WORTHY_____ of empowerment.

(2) Clearly lay out their _____MISSION AND RESPONSIBILITIES_____ .

(3) Verbally and visually show your _____SUPPORT_____ .

(4) Keep an _____OPEN DOOR_____ relationship with them.

(5) Give them the _____PUBLIC CREDIT_____ when successful.

STOP *and Assess*

To empower others, you must have power to give away. You must also be willing to give away the power, and you must find a worthy recipient to whom you can transfer the power.

The following questions will give you insight as to how well you work to empower others.

1. Is it easy to "share" your power and authority with others?

2. When you delegate a major responsibility to someone, do you attempt to pull it back and stay involved?

3. Are you training your key people?

4. Do you trust your key people?

5. Have you cultivated an environment that champions risk, allows mistakes and has an innovative spirit?

6. Do you consider yourself basically "secure" or "insecure" as a leader? How would those closest to you answer this question?

7. Do your key people express gratitude to you for the opportunities that you have made available for them?

Adopt the following guidelines as your very own in order to empower others.

1. **Let go!** When your organization was smaller you could personally lead and control the whole enterprise. With growth, however, you must learn to let go and trust others with responsibilities.

2. **Keep teaching, training and growing.** The best, most innovative, and fastest growing organizations have a generous budget for training their key personnel and the entire organization. Insist that new insights and information be applied to each person's area of responsibility.

3. **Give authority away.** When you keep your authority to yourself, your authority decreases. When you share your authority with others, it increases. If you give someone responsibility, you must give him or her the authority needed to fulfill the responsibility. This communicates trust and connects you with people.

4. **Care about and believe in people.** No matter how much experience you possess, your level of education or your title, people will believe in the leader when the leader believes in the people.

continued

The following guidelines will help you learn to care about a person:

- Look out for their best interests.

- Be honest with them even when it hurts.

- Believe in them. This is a statement of faith from your heart about their potential.

continued

An Influencer...

10. **R** <u>EPRODUCES</u> _____ other people

When you influence a child, you influence a _____<u>LIFE</u>_____ .

When you influence a parent, you influence a _____<u>FAMILY</u>_____ .

When you influence a worker, you influence a _____<u>COMPANY</u>_____ .

When you influence a leader, you influence everyone who looks to him or her for _____<u>LEADERSHIP</u>_____ .

We teach what we know—We reproduce who we are!

It takes a leader to *know* a leader.

It takes a leader to *show* a leader.

It takes a leader to *grow* a leader.

Q. "Why don't all leaders develop other leaders?"

(1) They are _____<u>INSECURE</u>_____ .

(2) They spend too much time with _____<u>FOLLOWERS</u>_____ .

(3) Followers are easier to find and lead than _____<u>LEADERS</u>_____ .

(4) They don't recognize the value of developing _____<u>LEADERS</u>_____ .

(5) Leadership has been viewed as a competitive _____<u>EFFORT</u>_____ , not a cooperative one.

It is one of the most beautiful compensations of this life that no man can sincerely try to help another without helping himself.

—Ralph Waldo Emerson

STOP *and Assess*

Are you reproducing other people through your influence as a leader? The following questions will help you decide:

1. Do you lean toward developing others or doing things yourself?

2. If you do not mentor well or consistently, what are some of the reasons?

3. Have you been personally mentored by someone?

4. Do you currently have a mentor? If so, what have you learned from your mentor in the last six months that you apply to your life today?

5. Does mentoring others fulfill or frustrate you?

6. Would others in your organization consider you a good mentor?

7. Can you list the names of those who would consider you their primary mentor, and who have gone on to mentor others?

You can be a great leader and still not raise up other leaders. The following principles will help you grow as a mentor so you can raise up other leaders around you.

1. Be genuinely interested in your students, and prove it through availability and commitment.

2. Begin by assessing the individual's strengths, weaknesses, commitment level, previous training, personal background and your expectation of the student. Wise mentors start at the level of their students, not above or below.

3. Listen more than you talk. The number one error made by most inexperienced mentors is to play the "great and wise teacher" and do all the talking.

4. Demonstrate integrity and high moral standards. You greatly lessen your ability to transfer what you know if your students do not buy into who you are as a person. Your life is more important than your lesson. (See examples on p. 37 in *Developing the Leader Within You* by John Maxwell.)

5. Don't "connect" your student to you in a needy way. This is stifling and unhealthy. An unhealthy dependency may be emotional or financial. Like a wise parent, mentor people with the goal in mind of one day setting them free to fly on their own.

continued

STOP

continued

6. Make your student think, reflect, self-examine and integrate new thoughts, lessons and ideas into everyday life. Don't give him or her all of the answers. Ask many questions to evoke his or her response and introspective thinking.

7. Both mentor and student should communicate their desires and expectations of the mentoring process.

8. Without desire from a student you are wasting your time. His or her desire is easily measured by their commitment to the mentoring process.

Can you think of someone who needs to be mentored by you?

Ask yourself:

Am I empowering people, or am I building my dream and using people to do it?

People must come first. Fred Smith says that Federal Express, from its inception, has put its people first because it is right to do so and because it is good business as well. "Our corporate philosophy is succinctly: People-Service-Profits."

You'll empower others by putting them above profit and gain.

To grow in this area, you may want to read *Becoming a Person of Influence* by Jim Dornan and John Maxwell. To order visit **www.INJOY.com** or call 1-800-333-6506.

Lesson Three

How to Grow as a Leader

Part One Overview

Introduce the Lesson   *(5 minutes)*

The opening quote on the video says it all; *It is the willingness and capacity to develop their skills that distinguishes leaders from followers* (Warren Bennis and Bert Nanus).

Today you will learn the key words that determine growth and the choices you must make in order to grow as a leader. Because this lesson focuses on the personal growth component of leadership, it will open up the door for great discussion on the choices we all make to better ourselves.

Watch the Lesson   *(25–35 minutes)*

Make sure everyone is comfortable and can see the screen easily; then show the video.

Group Discussion   *(15 minutes)*

1. Ask participants to complete this sentence: Something I can do today to grow personally is _____. Ask for volunteers to share their answers.

2. Ask participants the following: What is one thing within your organization that you are reluctant to change? Allow time for answers. Then ask, "Why?" Allow time for responses. Lead participants to think outside of the box to create new growth opportunities through change.

3. Have class members share things they find to be organization killers. (e.g., keeping business cards on the dash of the car, unopened mail stacks, etc.). Discuss necessary steps to improve the situation.

4. Ask if everyone will make a conscious decision to grow from this day forward.

Challenge   *(5 minutes)*

Ask each group member to set aside at least a half hour that week to complete the **Stop and Assess** exercises.

This lesson, in particular, means nothing if the student hasn't established a practical plan for implementation. Ask each participant to begin writing out his or her own personal growth plan. Remind them not to be overly ambitious, or they will never stick with it. Start simple and build.

Lesson Three

How to Grow as a Leader

Part One

It is the willingness *and capacity to develop their skills that distinguishes leaders from followers.*

—Warren Bennis and Bert Nanus

Growth is happiness!

The best leaders are ones who are passionate about personal growth.

Why stay we on earth except to grow?

—Robert Browning

Leadership can be taught. It is not something only for those born with innate leadership traits. There are at least four kinds of leaders:

1. The Leading Leader
2. The Learned Leader
3. The Latent Leader
4. The Limited Leader

(You can read more about each of these leaders in the Introduction of *Developing The Leader Within You* by John Maxwell.)

Three Words That Determine Growth

1. _____CHOICE_____—This allows me to _____START_____ growing.

   Growth is a personal choice. It is not an automatic process.

   What personal choices do you make that enable growth?

2. _____CHANGE_____—This allows me to _____KEEP_____ growing.

   Growth means change. If you plan to grow, plan to change.

   What changes have you made or will you make to facilitate growth?

3. _____CLIMATE_____—This allows me to _____ENJOY_____ growing.

   Our environment will be challenging and stimulating if we choose to grow.

   What's the weather like? Have you surrounded yourself with a growth atmosphere?

You cannot travel within and stand still without.

—James Allen

Choice: This allows me to start growing.

 **and Assess**

Have you chosen to grow? Answer the following questions to see how you rate in this area:

1. Do you have an intentional plan for personal leadership development that you are following on a regular basis? Where is this plan? Is it updated and current?

2. Have you received leadership training that has been helpful to you? What made the helpful training so valuable to you? How have you implemented the things you learned?

10 Choices Necessary to Grow as a Leader

1. Choose to be a _____LEADER_____ .

In every age there comes a time when a leader must come forward to meet the needs of the hour. Therefore, there is no potential leader who does not have the opportunity to make a positive difference in society. Tragically, there are times when a leader does not rise to the hour.

There is only one person who can choose if you are to be a leader: you. Your choice to do so involves action. You must choose to read, learn, study and associate with leaders.

Ask yourself: Am I hungry to grow as a leader?

Self-discipline is key for choosing to grow as a leader. A choice may be made in your heart and mind, but only the implementation of a plan will see results.

Use the following guidelines to become focused on self-discipline toward growth.

1. **Start small.** What you are going to be tomorrow, you are becoming today. It is essential to begin developing self-discipline in a small way today in order to be disciplined in a big way tomorrow.

2. **Start now.** As John Hancock Field says, *All worthwhile men have good thoughts, good ideas, and good intentions, but precious few of them ever translate those into action.*

3. **Organize your life.** When you are organized, you have a special power. You walk with a sure sense of purpose. Your priorities are clear in your mind. You move smoothly from one project to the next with no wasted motion.

Are you ready to begin? Can you:

    1. Begin today by starting small?

    2. Begin now with no procrastination?

    3. Organize your life in a clear and concise way?

2. Choose to start growing _____NOW_____ .

It's not what you are going to do, but it's what you are doing now that counts.

—Napoleon Hill

Why choose to start growing now?

A. Growth is not an _____AUTOMATIC_____ process.

B. This decision today will ensure a better _____TOMORROW_____ .

C. It is our _____RESPONSIBILITY_____ .

You've got to do your own growing, no matter how tall your grandfather is.

—Irish Proverb quoted by Warren Bennis, *On Becoming a Leader*

D. Your growth will determine your _____ORGANIZATION'S_____ growth.

Grow the organization and not the people = _____SHORT-TERM_____ growth.

Grow the organization and the people = _____LONG-TERM_____ growth.

Grow the organization, the people and the leaders = _____LIFELONG_____ growth.

 **and Assess**

Your personal growth will not happen unless you pursue it. Your future is determined by what you are doing now—at this moment—to become a leader.

If your personal growth is not an automatic process, yet it is your responsibility to ensure a better tomorrow and determine your organization's growth—what value do you put on your growth? Remember, your organization will not grow above you. You must continue to raise the bar through growth.

Begin today. Use your time wisely.

- Listen to tapes instead of the radio.

- Read books instead of watching TV.

- Involve your mind in active learning as much as possible.

3. Have a _____TEACHABLE_____ spirit.

It's what you learn after you know it all that counts.

—John Wooden

The greatest obstacle to discovery is not ignorance.

It is the illusion of knowledge.

 **STOP** *and Assess*

The day you become the Answer Man or Answer Woman is the day you stop learning. Keep the door open to learning!

Answer these questions to point you toward growth:

1. What new ideas or opinions have you recently ignored?

2. What new ideas or opinions can you pursue and consider?

3. What new habits can you exchange for old ones that will prove to be fresh and productive for your organization?

4. Focus on self-_____DEVELOPMENT_____ , not self-_____FULFILLMENT_____ .

Self-fulfillment means doing what I enjoy most and will receive the most strokes for doing. Self-development means doing what I am talented and uniquely fit to do, and that becomes my responsibility.

Self-fulfillment thinks of how something serves _____ME_____ .

Self-development thinks of how something helps me to serve _____OTHERS_____ .

With self-fulfillment, feeling good is the _____PRODUCT_____ .

With self-development, feeling good is the _____BY-PRODUCT_____ .

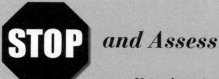 **and Assess**

Keep learning to develop your intellect, emotions and leadership. Your influence is greater when you challenge yourself because you challenge those within your organization.

Do you:—continually study?
　　　—keep information?
　　　—have a system to retrieve key information?

How can you organize information to enhance learning? List five organizational improvements that need to be made in your life:

(1) _____

(2) _____

(3) _____

(4) _____

(5) _____

5.　Never stay satisfied with _____ PRESENT _____ accomplishments.

A short verse by John Masefield:

And there were three men
Went down the road
As down the road went he.
The man they saw, the man he was,
And the man he wanted to be.

If what you did yesterday still looks big to you, you haven't done much today.

The day we become satisfied with our station in life is the day we stop growing.

 Remember, it takes time to grow. Start small and concentrate on today. The slow accumulation of disciplines will one day make a big difference.

What is one thing you can do today to keep you moving forward?

What are three things you can do habitually to keep you moving forward?

(1) _____

(2) _____

(3) _____

6. Be a _____ CONTINUAL _____ learner.

This guarantees that you will never stay satisfied with present accomplishments. Educators who don't learn new material can become stale. They can't grow because they don't continually learn.

Devote yourself to learning. Make learning a way of life for you, not an added extra.

Steps to Take:

1. Take five minutes at the end of each day to evaluate what you learned that day.

2. List at least three subjects of interest that you want to know more about.

3. Allow time to read or listen to tapes about these subjects.

4. Share what you learn with others.

 Sharing with others is an important part of continual learning. Through discussion and contemplation with others, your learning is reinforced. Your opinions and convictions take shape in concrete ways when ideas are discussed.

Name at least three people with whom you can share things you learn:

(1) _____

(2) _____

(3) _____

7. _____ CHANNEL _____ your learning to a few major themes.

C.S. Lewis said, *Every person is composed of a few themes.*

John Maxwell's Major Themes

(1) _____ RELATIONSHIPS _____ —This determines how well I know people.

(2) _____ ATTITUDE _____ —This determines how well I relate to people.

(3) _____ COMMUNICATION _____ —This determines how well I motivate people.

(4) _____ LEADERSHIP _____ —This determines how well I influence people.

(5) _____ PERSONAL GROWTH _____ —This determines how long I do all of the above!

 **and Assess**

The themes for your life will be uniquely your own. You must decide what you will pursue. Ask yourself:

- What are my gifts?

- What is my passion?

- What are my opportunities?

Using your answers to the above questions, list at least four of your life's themes. Seek to spend your time in those areas. Reflect on them, pursue them, read about them and study under knowledgeable people. Don't allow insignificant details or bits of unrelated information to blur your focus.

(1) _____

(2) _____

(3) _____

(4) _____

What will each of those themes determine?

Theme #1 will determine _____

_____

Theme #2 will determine _____

_____

Theme #3 will determine _____

_____

Theme #4 will determine _____

_____

The themes of your life will characterize you as a leader.

8. Develop a _____ PERSONAL _____ creed.

The value of a personal creed:

A. It spells out the concepts I accept as standards of my _THINKING AND BEHAVIOR_ .

B. It becomes a _____ COMPASS _____ for my life.

C. It helps me develop _____ HABITS _____ , which can turn into _____ REFLEXES _____ .

D. It helps me to _KNOW AND CONTRIBUTE_ to my uniqueness.

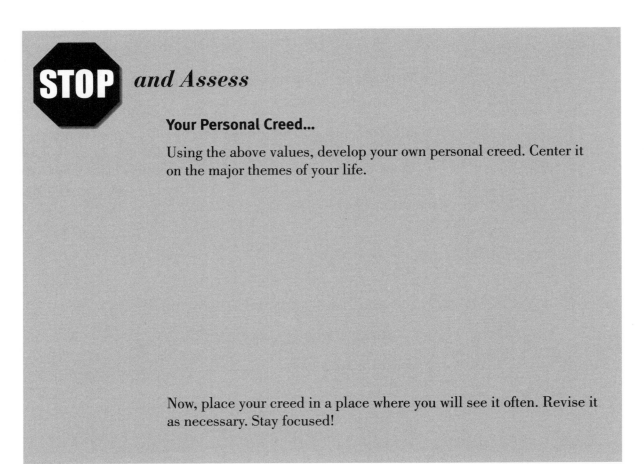

STOP *and Assess*

Your Personal Creed...

Using the above values, develop your own personal creed. Center it on the major themes of your life.

Now, place your creed in a place where you will see it often. Revise it as necessary. Stay focused!

9. Pay the _____ PRICE _____ .

For everything you gain, you lose something.

—Ralph Waldo Emerson

Price Tags of Personal Growth

(1) _____ DISCIPLINE _____   (4) _____ LONELINESS _____

(2) _____ RISK _____   (5) _____ TIME _____

(3) _____ CHANGE _____   (6) _____ MISUNDERSTANDING _____

*There has not yet been a person in our history who led a life of ease
whose name is worth remembering.*

—Theodore Roosevelt

STOP *and Assess*

Go back and review the price tags of personal growth. Are you
willing to pay these prices? To further consider the price of growth,
ask yourself the following:

1. Are you willing to work while others play?

2. Can you step out and take a chance?

3. Will you press on when others lose the vision and drop out?

4. Are you willing to give time to the process of growth?

Be candid with yourself. What areas will be the toughest for you?

Now list at least three things that you can forfeit or postpone in
order to spend more time in growth mode and less time in play
or procrastination.

(1) _____

(2) _____

(3) _____

10. Develop a _____SYSTEM_____ to apply what you learn.

Don't let your learning lead to knowledge. Let your learning lead to action.

—Jim Rohn

A. Develop a filing system.

B. File what you learn quickly.

   Advantages of filing:

   1. Reinforcement of what you learn

   2. Resources for future need

   3. You don't lose valuable resources—**#1 Time Waster**

   4. Helps you evaluate reading and authors

   5. Provides great material for teaching and writing

C. Apply what you learn quickly.

   Every day take one thing that you learned and ask yourself...

   1. *Where can I use this?*

   2. *When can I use this?*

   3. *Who needs to know this?*

   John Maxwell's system for application:

   1. Select one thing.

   2. Put it on a 3x5 card.

   3. Share it with spouse first.

   4. Share it with someone else within 24 hours.

   5. Put it in a lesson.

   6. Keep it visually in front of you for a week.

Change — This allows me to keep growing.

Something in human nature tempts us to stay where we're comfortable. We try to find a plateau, a resting place, where we have comfortable stress and adequate finances, where we have comfortable associations with people, without the intimidation of meeting new people and entering strange situations.

 **and Assess**

You can begin a filing system today. What will be your first
file folder?

Everything you read, see or hear has the potential to be in a folder!
Your collection will provide a wealth of resources and information.
These things will grow you!

For a resource that can help you grow in this area, check out *You Gotta have a System*—MIC Lesson.
Visit **www.INJOY.com** or call 1-800-333-6506.

Unless you try to do something beyond what you already mastered, you will never grow.
—Ronald E. Osborne

If we don't change, we don't grow. It we don't grow, we are not really living.
Growth demands a temporary surrender of security. It may mean a giving up of
familiar but limiting patterns, safe but unrewarding work, values no longer believed in,
relationships that have lost their meaning. As Dostoevsky put it, "Taking a new step,
uttering a new word, is what people fear most." The real fear should be the opposite course.
—Gail Sheehy, author

Lesson Three

How to Grow as a Leader

Part Two Overview

Introduce the Lesson *(5 minutes)*

This part of Lesson Three will challenge everyone in your group! Change is hard on everyone... sometimes hardest on a leader.

This week, as each participant learns how to create a healthy climate for growth, they will also learn the key elements to success—real success.

Let them know that today could be a defining moment for each person as they change their paradigm of success.

Watch the Lesson *(25–35 minutes)*

Make sure everyone is comfortable and can see the screen easily; then show the video.

Group Discussion *(15 minutes)*

1. Ask for volunteers to share personal experiences of paying the price. Encourage them to think of times they have postponed play and focused on the goal. Next, ask who has experienced the opposite experience and regretted his/her shortsighted vision.

2. Ask everyone to write down five things that they can immediately change in their own lives (allow a few minutes for them to write). They are welcome to share if they want, but this should be on a strictly volunteer basis.

3. Find out what kind of a growth environment exists in each person's workplace. Can it be improved? What can they do to improve it?

4. Remind the participants that today they learned that growth is a process—motivation gets you going and habits get you there. Ask, "What habits can you develop right now to facilitate the process of growth in your life?"

Challenge *(5 minutes)*

Ask each group member to set aside at least a half hour that week to complete the **Stop and Assess** exercises.

Last week each student should have started his or her own personal growth plan. Ask them to complete that plan this week and begin implementing it into their daily lives.

Lesson Three

How to Grow as a Leader

Part Two

Comments About Change:

(1) Start with _____YOURSELF_____ .

 The decision to change yourself begins with you—only you. The following questions will give you insight into your understanding that change begins with you.

1. Are you intentional or are you more random in your approach to life?

2. Are you moving forward?

3. What brought you this far?

The following words were written on the tomb of an Anglican Bishop (1100 A.D.) in the crypts of Westminster Abbey:

When I was young and free and my imagination had no limits, I dreamed of changing the world. As I grew older and wiser, I discovered the world would not change, so I shortened my sights somewhat and decided to change only my country. But it, too, seemed immovable.

As I grew into my twilight years, in one last desperate attempt, I settled for changing only my family, those closest to me, but alas, they would have none of it.

And now as I lie on my deathbed, I suddenly realize: If I had only changed myself first, then by example I would have changed my family.

From their inspiration and encouragement, I would then have been able to better my country and, who knows, I may have even changed the world.

(2) Failure to change at the right _____MOMENT_____ will provide the wrong _____RESULT_____ .

There is at least one point in the history of any company when you have to
change dramatically to rise to the next performance level.
Miss that moment, and you start to decline.

—Andrew S. Grove, Chairman, Intel

 **and Assess**

If you're not expecting or watching for key moments, they'll pass
right by you.

What are some key moments you've missed in life?

Take a moment to list key moments that you anticipate will happen
within your organization in the next six months.

How will you seize these moments?

Develop an eye that continually looks for key moments.

(3) Growth guarantees an exciting _____TOMORROW_____ .

Our growth and change opens many avenues and opportunities.

STOP *and Assess*

Think of at least one time that an opportunity opened to you as a result of your growth. The following may help you recall.

1. After attending a particular course or school, were you more qualified for specific positions?

2. What new opportunities have become available to you in the last year? How were they related to your growth and development?

3. Name three things you can do (read, listen to tapes, in-depth studies of your field, etc.) that could open new opportunities for you.

(1) _____

(2) _____

(3) _____

Climate: This allows me to enjoy growing.

The greatest of all miracles is that we need not be tomorrow what we are today, but we can improve if we make use of the potentials implanted in us by God.

—Rabbi Samuel M. Silver

How to Develop a Healthy Climate for Growth

1. Create a <u>GROWTH ENVIRONMENT</u> .

Fish will only grow to the size that their aquarium will accommodate. Given a larger space, they will grow larger.

A growth environment is a place where...

    1. Others are ahead of you.

    2. You are still challenged.

    3. Your focus is forward.

    4. The atmosphere is affirming.

    5. You are out of your comfort zone.

    6. You wake up excited.

    7. You don't fear failure.

    8. Others are growing.

    9. There is a willingness to change.

    10. Growth is modeled and expected.

 **STOP** *and Assess*

This is a good time for you to stop and make a game plan. Design a chart that portrays growth. Use the ten growth environment enhancers listed above to make two diagrams: one to chart your current growth and one to chart your ideal growth.

First, picture your current growth environment for a typical week, factoring in all ten growth environment enhancers. Is it nonexistent? Is it weak? Is it leading you to grow daily? Diagram a typical Monday through Friday. Does Monday start off strong and then you taper off? Ten represents a peak environment for learning and one represents a growth environment that is non-existent.

	Monday	Tuesday	Wednesday	Thursday	Friday
10					
9					
8					
7					
6					
5					
4					
3					
2					
1					

STOP

continued

Second, diagram your desired growth environment. Chart an ideal course for optimum growth. This may take some time, but without a plan you won't grow. Invest the time now.

	Monday	Tuesday	Wednesday	Thursday	Friday
10					
9					
8					
7					
6					
5					
4					
3					
2					
1					

List specific ingredients needed to create your optimum growth climate.

(1) _____

(2) _____

(3) _____

2. Develop relationships with ___GROWING PEOPLE___ .

It's not always comfortable, but always profitable,
to associate with people larger than ourselves.

—John Maxwell

Emerson and Thoreau's questions to each other when they met: *And what has become clearer to you since last we met?*

Growing together provides...

A. Increased Insight

B. Shared Joy

C. Accountability

D. Future Relationship

E. Shared Vision

F. Worthwhile Conversation

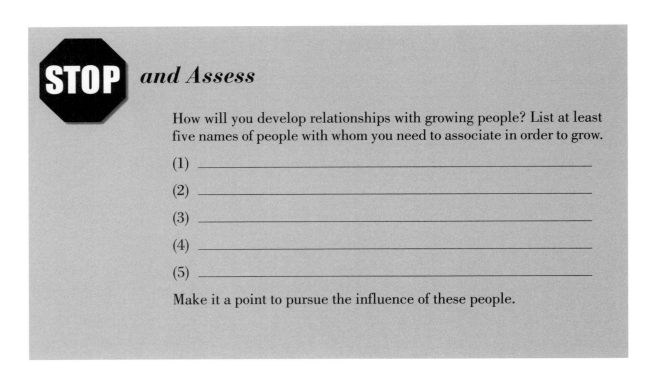

STOP *and Assess*

How will you develop relationships with growing people? List at least five names of people with whom you need to associate in order to grow.

(1) _____

(2) _____

(3) _____

(4) _____

(5) _____

Make it a point to pursue the influence of these people.

3. Understand that growth is a _____PROCESS_____ , not an _____EVENT_____ .

Motivation gets you going.

Habits get you there.

You will never change your life until you change something you do daily. The secret of your future is hidden in your daily routine.

Growth is not an automatic process! It is determined by the . . .

   Choices we make

   Changes we make

   Climate we create

INJOY® has two resources to help you grow in this area: *The Success Journey* and *Success One Day at a Time.* You can purchase these resources by visiting **www.INJOY.com** or calling 1-800-333-6506.

STOP *and Assess*

Examine a typical day in your life. Look for areas to include life changing, growth opportunities. Maybe you have an hour or more a day that "falls through the cracks." Include practices that will help you produce growth.

What daily choices do you make concerning time and how it is spent?

What daily changes can you make to better utilize your time (e.g., get coffee from home instead of the 15-minute stop each morning, get up 15 minutes earlier, etc.)?

How to Be a REAL Success

Relationships
- *Be a People Person*
- *Becoming a Person of Influence*
- *The Power of Influence*
- *The Power of Partnership*
- *The Treasure of a Friend*

Equipping
- *Developing the Leaders Around You*
- *Partners in Prayer*
- *The 17 Indisputable Laws of Teamwork* (Fall 2001)
- *Success One Day at a Time*

Attitude
- *The Winning Attitude*
- *Failing Forward*
- *Think on These Things*

Leadership
- *The 21 Indispensable Qualities of a Leader*
- *The 21 Irrefutable Laws of Leadership*
- *The 21 Most Powerful Minutes in a Leader's Day*
- *Developing the Leader Within You*
- *The Power of Leadership*
- *The Right to Lead*

All of these resources are available by visiting www.INJOY.com or calling 1-800-333-6506.

Lesson Four

Reflections of a Leader

Part One Overview

Introduce the Lesson   *(5 minutes)*

Encourage your group; average people with average dreams who live average lives don't work through a process like this. They have the potential to achieve meaningful accomplishments in life. If everyone sticks with the process, the investment into personal growth will be not only worthwhile, but also rewarding.

As they will learn today, taking time to reflect creates a valuable future. As they look back with John Maxwell over his leadership reflections, they have a unique opportunity to learn from someone else's successes and failures.

Courage is one essential that will be covered today. Share a time when it took courage for you to make a hard call, and after the video share the outcome of making that tough decision.

Watch the Lesson   *(25–35 minutes)*

Make sure everyone is comfortable and can see the screen easily; then show the video.

Group Discussion   *(15 minutes)*

1. Have class members describe to the group (by personality traits, not by name) a person to whom he or she is drawn. Ask someone in the class to keep a list of the qualities named. What qualities are most popular? Do participants see these qualities in themselves?

2. Ask each person to evaluate for themselves if they would want to attract people like they are. Would they want to reproduce leaders like themselves? What do they need to change now to become more like someone they would want to attract or reproduce?

3. Have everyone discuss an instance when it took great courage for him or her to make a decision. What was the outcome?

Challenge   *(5 minutes)*

Ask each group member to set aside at least a half hour that week to complete the **Stop and Assess** exercises.

Make sure that each person has completed reading the *Developing the Leader Within You* book.

Ask every person to prepare any questions that they would like to ask the group next week, in your last meeting time.

Section Four
Reflections of a Leader
Part One

Ten years ago my subject for INJOY Life Club® subscribers was "I'm 40 and Counting."
Today, ten years later, I'm willing to look back, not because my race has been run,
but because I want to help others run successfully. Yesterday, my success in running life's
race was at the top of my list. Today, I feel like Paul who said,
"Keep track of those you see running this same course, headed for the same goal."
(Phil. 3:16) We live life looking forward but we understand it looking backward.

—John Maxwell

Results of Reflection Time

1. It allows us to have second thoughts… _____ FIRST _____ .

   To ponder, consider, think and pray

2. Over time…the important and the unimportant _____ SEPARATE _____ .

   No other entity works as well as time in teaching us

3. Only time will allow us to journey from the "know how" of leadership to the "know why" of leadership.

   The application of important principles becomes actual understanding

The Five Stages of Leadership Knowledge

1. Know _____ HOW _____ to lead—This deals with _____ WARNING _____ and _____ GROWTH _____ .
2. Know _____ WHO _____ to lead—This deals with _____ COMMUNITY _____ and _____ TEAMWORK _____ .
3. Know _____ WHERE _____ to lead—This deals with _____ CALLING _____ and _____ VISION _____ .
4. Know _____ WHEN _____ to lead—This deals with _____ TIMING _____ and _____ EFFECTIVENESS _____ .
5. Know _____ WHY _____ to lead—This deals with _____ MOTIVES _____ and _____ SECURITY _____ .

Reflection #1: People become like their _____ LEADER _____ .

    I teach what I _____ KNOW _____ .

    I reproduce what I _____ AM _____ .

The Law of Magnetism: We attract who we *are* not who we *want*.

STOP *and Assess*

This brief exercise will give you insight as to how well you are living the Law of Magnetism.

1. How would you describe the people you are attracting to yourself?

2. What are your greatest personal assets that contribute to attracting others in a positive way?

3. What are possible problematic areas of your life that could cause the Law of Magnetism to work against what you desire to accomplish?

4. Are the people you attract today of a higher caliber than those you attracted a year or two ago?

5. Do you attract skilled and talented people?

Lessons to Be Learned

1. It will take a conscious effort to _____ APPRECIATE _____ and _____ ATTRACT _____ people who are different than the leadership.

2. The people tend to have the same _____ STRENGTHS _____ and _____ WEAKNESSES _____ of their leadership.

3. The leadership of the organization must change _____ BEFORE _____ the people.

    Remember, people _____ DO _____ what people _____ SEE _____ .

Reflection #2: Leading others takes _____COURAGE_____ .

Knowing the right decision is _____EASY_____ .

Making the right decision is _____HARD_____ .

Lessons to Be Learned

1. A leader is responsible to place the interests of the organization _____FIRST_____ .

2. Each courageous call required much _____TIME, ENERGY_____ and _____POWER_____ .

3. Each courageous call demanded _____RISK_____ .

4. Each courageous call was _____QUESTIONED_____ and _____CRITICIZED_____ .

5. Each courageous call _____COST ME GREATLY_____ .

6. Each courageous call _____LIFTED_____ me to a higher lever.

Tough calls = _____BREAKTHROUGHS_____

It's lonely at the top… so you better know why you are there.

Lesson Four

Reflections of a Leader

Part Two Overview

Introduce the Lesson *(5 minutes)*

You made it! You are on your last lesson and this should be a celebration. Each person has made a commitment to grow over the past eight weeks and has fulfilled that commitment well.

Appropriately, this week covers teamwork and adding value to other people. Hopefully, even as a class, you have learned to work together as a team—encouraging and motivating each other.

Take time this week to express your appreciation again for each person. Possibly, publicly acknowledge a few specific people that you have observed substantial growth in.

Watch the Lesson *(25–35 minutes)*

Make sure everyone is comfortable and can see the screen easily; then show the video.

Group Discussion *(15 minutes)*

1. Read through the Laws of Teamwork again. Ask each person to rate on a scale from 1 to 10 where they rate on each law.

2. Ask for volunteers who will share about a time when they failed or made a mistake and admitted it to people within their organization. Carry the discussion through to talk about how it affected the individual sharing and those around him or her.

3. Ask, "What are you doing right now to add value to the people around you?"

4. Ask, "If you were stripped of your title, would your leadership be affected? Why or why not?"

5. As a group, discuss the top three things that they will take away from this course and if they thought of any questions that they have for you or for the other members.

Challenge *(5 minutes)*

It's the last time—make sure everyone finishes strong. Ask each group member to set aside at least a half hour that week to complete the **Stop and Assess** exercises.

Thank them again for their dedication to learning and for supporting the class.

Section Four

Reflections of a Leader

Part Two

Reflection #3: _____ TEAM _____ **leadership is more effective than** _____ INDIVIDUAL _____ **leadership.**

Laws of Teamwork

1. The Law of the _____ LONE RANGER _____ —One is too small of a number to achieve lasting significance.

2. The Law of the _____ BENCH _____ —Great teams have depth.

3. The Law of the _____ NICHE _____ —Each player has a place where they add the most value.

4. The Law of _____ MT. EVEREST _____ —As the challenge increases, the need for teamwork increases.

5. The Law of the _____ CHAIN _____ —The strength of the team is impacted by its weakest link.

6. The Law of _____ DIVIDENDS _____ —Investing in the team compounds over time.

Reflection #4: _____ ADVERSITY _____ **when I handled it** _____ CORRECTLY _____ **, helped me become a better** _____ PERSON _____ **and** _____ LEADER _____ **.**

At the moment of adversity we usually fail to see or appreciate the benefits.

After adversity has passed, over a period of time we see and appreciate the benefits…
if we have responded correctly.

The major difference between average people and achieving people is their perception of and response to failure. (Thesis of *Failing Forward* book by John Maxwell)

You will have a "train wreck." The questions are:

1) When will you have it?

2) How will you respond?

Adversity will come! Sometimes we know it's around the corner and other times it hits totally unannounced. Either way, you need to be prepared for adversity.

STOP *and Assess*

An individual is one link. A group of individuals forms a chain that provides strength, purpose and togetherness. As a leader, seek to build a strong team. Give the players opportunities to work together, build together and strategize together.

Name at least three activities you can schedule that will promote teamwork among the members of your organization.

(1) _____

(2) _____

(3) _____

Is your current team winning or losing?

The following will allow you to contemplate your response to unexpected curves in the road and consider ways to be prepared.

When tough times hit, will you:

1. Continue with your dream or let it fall apart?

2. Readjust your goals or assume you've failed?

3. Use the time to positively or negatively influence others?

4. Seek to maintain organization?

5. View the adversity as a problem solving activity or as a destructive force that has ruined your hopes?

6. Take risks in order to go around, above, through or under the problem?

7. Think creatively toward a solution?

continued

STOP

continued

Imagine that your organization lost two key people to other organizations in a two-week period. During that same time, your doctor advised you to stay off of your feet for five days because of a recurring back injury. Another key person is scheduled for surgery during this time and will be out for six weeks. It looks like things are falling apart.

Use these key words to plot a winning strategy to overcome the adversity and come out of it a stronger leader.

Dreams

Goals

Influence

Personal Organization

Prioritize

Problem-Solve

Risks

Decisions

Creativity

Write your plan here.

Lessons I've Learned From a Heart Attack

1) I've learned to be _____GRATEFUL_____ for life.

I have often thought it would be a blessing if each human being were stricken blind and deaf for a few days during his early adult life. Darkness would make him more appreciative of sight; silence would teach him the joys of sound.

—Helen Keller

2) I've learned that you can never tell people you love that you love them _____ENOUGH_____.

3) I'm learning to be a _____GOOD_____ steward of my body.

4) I've learned the grace of _____RECEIVING_____ .

5) I've learned again the value of _____PRAYER_____ .

6) I've learned to focus on what I have, not on what I _____HAVE LOST_____ .

7) I've learned that _____DEVELOPING_____ a solid INJOY® team has paid off.

8) I've learned to place my family _____FIRST_____ .

9) I've learned that God still has plans for my life.

Success is having those who are closest to me love and respect me the most.

Here is a test to find whether your mission on earth is finished. If you're alive, it isn't.

—Richard Bach

Review: Reflections of a Leader

1. People become like their leader.

2. Leading others takes courage.

3. Team leadership is more effective than individual leadership.

4. Adversity, when handled correctly, helps me become a better person.

Reflection #5: Great leaders _____ ADD VALUE _____ **to the people they serve.**

Success is...

_____ KNOWING _____ my purpose in life

_____ GROWING _____ to my maximum potential

_____ SOWING _____ seeds that benefit others

~

To be successful is to be helpful, caring and constructive, to make everything and everyone you touch a little bit better. The best thing you have to give is yourself.

—Norman Vincent Peale

~

How to Add Value to Others

1. We add value to others when we truly _____ VALUE THEM _____ .

   When we truly value people we...

   A. _____ BELIEVE _____ in them BEFORE they believe in us.

   B. _____ SERVE _____ them BEFORE they serve us.

~

The purpose of life is not to win. The purpose of life is to grow and to share. When you come to look back on all that you have done in life, you will get more satisfaction from the pleasure you have brought into other people's lives than you will from the times that you outdid and defeated them.

—Rabbi Harold Kushner

~

   C. _____ WE DRAW OTHERS TO US _____ .

   You will always move toward anyone who increases you and away from anyone who makes you less.

2. We add value to others when we _____ MAKE OURSELVES _____ more valuable.

~

In order to do more, I've got to be more.

—Jim Rohn

~

3. We add value to others when we _____ KNOW _____ and _____ RELATE _____ to what they value.

Need More Workbooks?

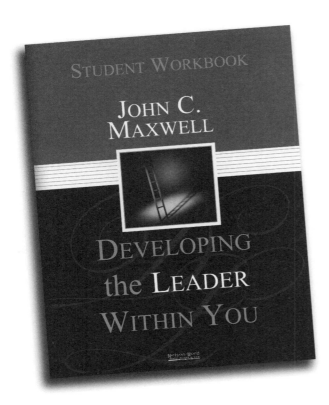

Visit
www.INJOY.com

Or call
1-800-333-6506

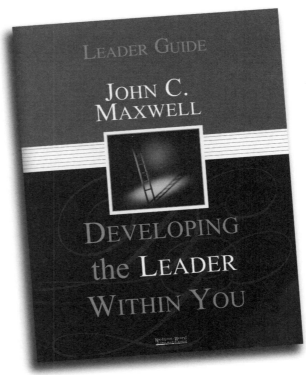

Conclusion

I promised when you started this journey that you would see a difference in your life as you learned to apply these principles. My prayer is that you have not only enjoyed this process, but that you also have seen a difference in your life.

You are a winner and you will make a difference.

Never stop growing!

John C. Maxwell